The Fatal Falsehood by Hannah More

Hannah More was born on February 2nd, 1745 at Fishponds in the parish of Stapleton, near Bristol. She was the fourth of five daughters.

The City of Bristol, at that time, was a centre for slave-trading and Hannah would, over time, become one of its staunchest critics.

She was keen to learn, possessed a sharp intellect and was assiduous in studying. Hannah first wrote in 1762 with The Search after Happiness (by the mid-1780s some 10,000 copies had been sold).

In 1767 Hannah became engaged to William Turner. After six years, with no wedding in sight, the engagement was broken off. Turner then bestowed upon her an annual annuity of £200. This was enough to meet her needs and set her free to pursue a literary career.

Her first play, The Inflexible Captive, was staged at Bath in 1775. The famous David Garrick himself produced her next play, Percy, in 1777 as well as writing both the Prologue and Epilogue for it. It was a great success when performed at Covent Garden in December of that year.

Hannah turned to religious writing with Sacred Dramas in 1782; it rapidly ran through nineteen editions. These and the poems Bas-Bleu and Florio (1786) mark her gradual transition to a more serious and considered view of life.

Hannah contributed much to the newly-founded Abolition Society including, in February 1788, her publication of Slavery, a Poem recognised as one of the most important of the abolition period.

Her work now became more evangelical. In the 1790s she wrote several Cheap Repository Tracts which covered moral, religious and political topics and were both for sale or distributed to literate poor people. The most famous is, perhaps, The Shepherd of Salisbury Plain, describing a family of incredible frugality and contentment. Two million copies of these were circulated, in one year.

In 1789, she purchased a small house at Cowslip Green in Somerset. She was instrumental in setting up twelve schools in the area by 1800.

She continued to oppose slavery throughout her life, but at the time of the Abolition Bill of 1807, her health did not permit her to take as active a role in the movement as she had done in the late 1780s, although she maintained a correspondence with Wilberforce and others.

In July 1833, the Bill to abolish slavery throughout the British Empire passed in the House of Commons, followed by the House of Lords on August 1st.

Hannah More died on September 7th, 1833.

Index of Contents
DRAMATIS PERSONAE

DRAMATIS PERSONÆ

Earl GUILDFORD,	Mr. Clarke.
RIVERS, his Son,	Mr. Lewis.
ORLANDO, a young Italian Count,	Mr. Wroughton.
BERTRAND,	Mr. Aickin.
EMMELINA,	Miss Younge.
JULIA,	Mrs. Hartley.

SCENE—Earl Guildford's Castle

PROLOGUE

Our modern poets now can scarcely choose
A subject worthy of the Tragic Muse;
For bards so well have glean'd th' historic field,
That scarce one sheaf th' exhausted ancients yield;
Or if, perchance, they from the golden crop
Some grains, with hand penurious, rarely drop;
Our author these consigns to manly toil,
For classic themes demand a classic soil,
A vagrant she, the desert waste who chose,
Where Truth and History no restraints impose.
To her the wilds of fiction open lie,
A flow'ry prospect, and a boundless sky;

Yet hard the task to keep the onward way,
Where the wide scenery lures the foot to stray;
Where no severer limits check the Muse,
Than lawless fancy is dispos'd to choose.
Nor does she emulate the loftier strains
Which high heroic Tragedy maintains:
Nor conquests she, nor wars, nor triumphs sings,
Nor with rash hand o'erturns the thrones of kings.
No ruin'd empires greet to night your eyes,
No nations at our bidding fall or rise;
To statesmen deep, to politicians grave,
These themes congenial to their tastes we leave.
Of crowns and camps, a kingdom's weal or woe,
How few can judge, because how few can know!
But here you all may boast the censor's art;
Here all are critics who possess a heart.
Of the mix'd passions we display to-night,
Each hearer judges like the Stagyrite.
The scenes of private life our author shows,
A simple story of domestic woes;
Nor unimportant is the glass we hold,
To show th' effect of passions uncontroll'd;
To govern empires is the lot of few,
But all who live have passions to subdue.
Self-conquest is the lesson books should preach,
Self-conquest is the theme the Stage should teach.
Vouchsafe to learn this obvious duty here,
The verse though feeble, yet the moral's clear.
O mark to-night the unexampled woes
Which from unbounded self-indulgence flows.
Your candour once endur'd our author's lays,
Endure them now—it will be ample praise.

THE FATAL FALSEHOOD

ACT I

SCENE—An Apartment in Guildford Castle

Enter **BERTRAND**

BERTRAND
What fools are serious melancholy villains!
I play a surer game, and screen my heart
With easy looks and undesigning smiles;

And while my plots still spring from sober thought,
My deeds appear th' effect of wild caprice,
And I the thoughtless slave of giddy chance.
What but this frankness could have won the promise
Of young Orlando, to confide to me
That secret grief which preys upon his heart?
'Tis shallow, indiscreet hypocrisy
To seem too good: I am the careless Bertrand,
The honest, undesigning, plain, blunt man.
The follies I avow cloak those I hide;
For who will search where nothing seems conceal'd?
'Tis rogues of solid, prudent, grave demeanour
Excite suspicion; men on whose dark brow
Discretion, with his iron hand, has grav'd
The deep-mark'd characters of thoughtfulness.
Here comes my uncle, venerable Guildford,
Whom I could honour, were he not the sire
Of that aspiring boy, who fills the gap
'Twixt me and fortune: Rivers, how I hate thee!

[Enter **GUILDFORD**

How fares my noble uncle?

GUILFORD
Honest Bertrand!
I must complain we have so seldom met:
Where do you keep? believe me, we have miss'd you.

BERTRAND
O, my good lord! your pardon—spare me, sir,
For there are follies in a young man's life,
Vain schemes and thoughtless hours which I should blush
To lay before your wise and temperate age.

GUILFORD
Well, be it so—youth has a privilege,
And I should be asham'd could I forget
I have myself been young, and harshly chide
This not ungraceful gaiety. Yes, Bertrand,
Prudence becomes moroseness, when it makes
A rigid inquisition of the fault,
Not of the man, perhaps, but of his youth.
Foibles that shame the head on which old Time
Has shower'd his snow are then more pardonable,
And age has many a weakness of its own.

BERTRAND

Your gentleness, my lord, and mild reproof,
Correct the wand'rings of misguided youth,
More than rebuke, and shame me into virtue.

GUILFORD
Saw you my beauteous ward, the Lady Julia?

BERTRAND
She past this way, and with her your fair daughter,
Your Emmelina.

GUILFORD
Call them both my daughters;
For scarce is Emmelina more belov'd
Than Julia, the dear child of my adoption.
The hour approaches too, (and bless it, heav'n,
With thy benignest kindliest influence!)
When Julia shall indeed become my daughter,
Shall, in obedience to her father's will,
Crown the impatient vows of my brave son,
And richly pay him for his dangers past.

BERTRAND
Oft have I wonder'd how the gallant Rivers,
Youthful and ardent, doting to excess,
Could dare the dangers of uncertain war,
Ere marriage had confirm'd his claim to Julia.

GUILFORD
'Twas the condition of her father's will,
My brave old fellow-soldier, and my friend!
He wish'd to see our ancient houses join'd
By this, our children's union; but the veteran
So highly valued military prowess,
That he bequeath'd his fortunes and his daughter
To my young Rivers, on these terms alone,
That he should early gain renown in arms;
And if he from the field return'd a conqueror,
That sun which saw him come victorious home
Should witness their espousals. Yet he comes not!
The event of war is to the brave uncertain,
Nor can desert in arms ensure success.

BERTRAND
Yet fame speaks loudly of his early valour.

GUILFORD
Ere since th' Italian Count, the young Orlando,

My Rivers' bosom friend, has been my guest,
The glory of my son is all his theme:
Oh! he recounts his virtues with such joy,
Dwells on his merit with a zeal so warm,
As to his gen'rous heart pays back again
The praises he bestows.

BERTRAND
Orlando's noble.
He's of a tender, brave, and gallant nature,
Of honour most romantic, with such graces
As charm all womankind.

GUILFORD
And here comes one,
To whom the story of Orlando's praise
Sounds like sweet music.

BERTRAND
What, your charming daughter!
Yes, I suspect she loves th' Italian Count: [Aside.
That must not be. Now to observe her closely.

[Enter **EMMELINA**.

GUILFORD
Come hither, Emmelina: we were speaking
Of the young Count Orlando. What think you
Of this accomplish'd stranger?

EMMELINA (confused)
Of Orlando?
Sir, as my father's guest, my brother's friend,
I do esteem the Count.

GUILFORD
Nay, he has merit
Might justify thy friendship if he wanted
The claims thou mention'st; yet I mean to blame him.

EMMELINA
What has he done? How has he wrong'd my father?
For you are just, and are not angry lightly;
And he is mild, unapt to give offence,
As you to be offended.

GUILFORD
Nay, 'tis not much:

But why does young Orlando shun my presence?
Why lose that cheerful and becoming spirit
Which lately charm'd us all? Rivers will chide us,
Should he return, and find his friend unhappy.
He is not what he was. What says my child?

EMMELINA
My lord, when first my brother's friend arriv'd—
Be still, my heart. [Aside.

BERTRAND
She dares not use his name.
Her brother's friend! [Aside.

EMMELINA
When first your noble guest
Came from that voyage, he kindly undertook
To ease our terrors for my Rivers' safety,
When we believ'd him dead; he seem'd most happy,
And shar'd the gen'ral joy his presence gave.
Of late he is less gay; my brother's absence
(Or I mistake) disturbs his friend's repose:
Nor is it strange; one mind informs them both;
Each is the very soul that warms the other,
And both are wretched, or are bless'd together.

BERTRAND
Why trembles my fair cousin?

EMMELINA
Can I think
That my lov'd brother's life has been in danger,
Nor feel a strong emotion?

BERTRAND (ironically)
Generous pity!
But when that danger has so long been past,
You should forget your terrors.

EMMELINA
I shall never.
For when I think that danger sprung from friendship;
That Rivers, to preserve another's life,
Incurr'd this peril, still my wonder rises.

BERTRAND
And why another's life? Why not Orlando's?
Such caution more betrays than honest freedom.

GUILFORD

He's still the same, the gibing, thoughtless Bertrand,
Severe of speech, but innocent of malice.

[Exit **GUILDFORD**: **EMMELINA** going.

BERTRAND

Stay, my fair cousin! still with adverse eyes
Am I beheld? Had I Orlando's form,
I mean, were I like him, your brother's friend,
Then would your looks be turn'd thus coldly on me?

EMMELINA

But that I know your levity means nothing,
And that your heart accords not with your tongue,
This would offend me.

BERTRAND

Come, confess the truth,
That this gay Florentine, this Tuscan rover,
Has won your easy heart, and given you his:
I know the whole; I'm of his secret council;
He has confess'd—

EMMELINA

Ha! what has he confess'd?

BERTRAND

That you are wond'rous fair: nay, nothing further:
How disappointment fires her angry cheek! [Aside.
Yourself have told the rest, your looks avow it;
Your eyes are honest, they conceal no secrets.

EMMELINA

Know, Sir, that virtue no concealment needs:
So far from dreading, she solicits notice,
And wishes every secret thought she harbours
Bare to the eye of men, as 'tis to Heav'n.

BERTRAND

Yet mark me well: trust not Orlando's truth;
The citron groves have heard his amorous vows
Breath'd out to many a beauteous maid of Florence;
Bred in those softer climes, his roving heart
Ne'er learn'd to think fidelity a virtue:
He laughs at tales of British constancy.
But see, Orlando comes—he seeks you here.

With eyes bent downwards, folded arms, pale cheeks
Disorder'd looks, and negligent attire,
And all the careless equipage of love,
He bends this way. Why does the mounting blood
Thus crimson your fair cheek? He does not see us—
I'll venture to disturb his meditations,
And instantly return.

[Exit **BERTRAND**.

EMMELINA
No more; but leave me.
He's talkative but harmless, rude but honest;
Fuller of mirth than mischief.—See they meet—
This way they come: why am I thus alarm'd?
What is't to me that here Orlando comes?
Oh for a little portion of that art
Ungenerous men ascribe to our whole sex!
A little artifice were prudence now:
But I have none; my poor unpractis'd heart
Is so unknowing of dissimulation,
So little skill'd to seem the thing it is not,
That if my lips are mute my looks betray me.

[Re-enter **BERTRAND** with **ORLANDO**.

BERTRAND
Now to alarm her heart, and search out his.   [Aside.

ORLANDO
We crave your pardon, beauteous Emmelina,
If rudely we intrude upon your thoughts;
Thoughts pure as infants' dreams or angels' wishes,
And gentle as the breast from which they spring.

EMMELINA
Be still, my heart, nor let him see thy weakness.   [Aside.
We are much bound to thank you, cousin Bertrand,
That since your late return the Count Orlando
Appears once more among us.—Say, my lord,
Why have you shunn'd your friends' society?
Was it well done? My father bade me chide you;
I am not made for chiding, but he bade me:
He says, no more you rise at early dawn
With him to chase the boar: I pleaded for you;
Told him 'twas savage sport.

ORLANDO

What was his answer?

EMMELINA
He said 'twas sport for heroes, and made heroes;
That hunting was the very school of war,
Taught our brave youth to shine in nobler fields,
Preserv'd 'em from the rust of dull inaction,
Trained 'em for arms, and fitted them for conquest.

ORLANDO
O, my fair advocate! scarce can I grieve
To have done wrong, since my offence has gain'd
So sweet a pleader.

BERTRAND (aside.)
So, I like this well;
Full of respect, but cold.

EMMELINA
My Lord, your pardon;
My father waits my coming: I attend him.

[Exit.

BERTRAND
In truth, my Lord, you're a right happy man;
Her parting look proclaims that you are bless'd;
The crimson blushes on her cheek display'd
A gentle strife 'twixt modesty and love:
Discretion strove to dash the rising joy,
But conquering love prevail'd and told the tale.
My Lord, you answer not.

ORLANDO
What shall I say?
Oh, couldst thou read my heart!

BERTRAND
The hour is come
When my impatient friendship claims that trust
Which I so oft have press'd, and you have promis'd.

ORLANDO
I cannot tell thee; 'tis a tale of guilt:
How shall I speak? my resolution sickens;
All virtuous men will shun me; thou wilt scorn me,
And fly the foul contagion of my crime.

BERTRAND

My bosom is not steel'd with that harsh prudence
Which would reproach thy failings; tell me all:
The proudest heart loves to repose its faults
Upon a breast that has itself a tincture
Of human weakness: I have frailties too,
Frailties that teach me how to pity thine.
What! silent still? Thou lov'st my beauteous cousin!
Have I not guess'd?

ORLANDO

I own that she has charms
Might warm a frozen stoic into love,
Tempt hermits back again to that bad world
They had renounc'd, and make religious men
Forgetful of their holy vows to heaven:
Yet, Bertrand—come, I'll tell thee all my weakness;
Thou hast a tender, sympathising heart—
Thou art not rigid to a friend's defects.
That heavenly form I view with eyes as cold
As marble images of lifeless saints:
I see, and know the workmanship divine;
My judgment owns her exquisite perfections;
But my rebellious heart denies her claim.

BERTRAND

What do I hear! you love her not!

ORLANDO

Oh, Bertrand!
For pity do not hate me: but thou must;
For am I not at variance with myself?
Yet shall I wrong her gentle trusting nature,
And spurn the heart I labour'd to obtain?
She loves me, Bertrand; oh, too sure she loves me;
Loves me with tenderest, truest, chastest passion;
Loves me, oh, barbarous fate! as I love—Julia.

BERTRAND

Heard I aright? Did you not speak of Julia?
Julia, the lovely ward of my good uncle?
Julia! the mistress of your friend, of Rivers?

ORLANDO

Go on, go on, and urge me with my guilt;
Display my crime in all its native blackness:
Tell me some legend of infernal falsehood,
Tell me some dreadful tale of perjur'd friends,

Of trust betray'd, of innocence deceiv'd:
Place the dire chronicle before my eyes;
Inflame the horror, aggravate the guilt,—
That I may see the evils which await me;
Nor pull such fatal mischiefs on my head,
As with my ruin must involve the fate
Of all I love on earth.

BERTRAND

Just as I wish. [Aside.

ORLANDO

Thou know'st I left my native Italy,
Directed hither by the noble Rivers,
To ease his father's fears, who thought he fell
In that engagement where we both were wounded:
His was a glorious wound, gain'd in the cause
Of gen'rous friendship; for an hostile spear,
Aim'd at my breast, Rivers in his receiv'd,
Saved my devoted life, and won my soul.

BERTRAND

So far I knew; but what of Emmelina?

ORLANDO

Whether her gentle beauties first allur'd me,
Or whether peaceful scenes and rural shades,
Or leisure, or the want of other objects,
Or solitude, apt to engender love,
Engag'd my soul, I know not; but I lov'd her.
We were together always, till the habit
Grew into something like necessity.
When Emmelina left me I was sad,
Nor knew a joy till Emmelina came;
Her soft society amus'd my mind,
Fill'd up my vacant heart, and touch'd my soul:
'Twas gratitude, 'twas friendship, 'twas esteem,
'Twas reason, 'twas persuasion,—nay, 'twas love.

BERTRAND

But where was Julia?

ORLANDO

Oh, too soon she came:
For when I saw that wondrous form of beauty,
I stood entranc'd, like some astronomer,
Who, as he views the bright expanse of heaven,
Finds a new star. I gaz'd and was undone;

Gaz'd, and forgot the tender Emmelina;
Gaz'd, and forgot the gen'rous, trusting Rivers;
Forgot my faith, my friendship, and my honour.

BERTRAND
Does Julia know your love?

ORLANDO
Forbid it, heaven!
What! think'st thou I am so far gone in guilt
As boldly to avow it? Bertrand, no;
For all the kingdoms of the spacious earth
I would not wrong my friend, or damn my honour.

BERTRAND
Trust me, you judge too hardly of yourself.

ORLANDO
Think I have lodg'd a secret in thy breast
On which my peace, my fame, my all depends:
Long have I struggled with the fatal truth,
And scarce have dared to breathe it to myself;
For, oh, too surely the first downward step,
The treacherous path that leads to guilty deeds,
Is to make sin familiar to the thoughts.

[Exit.

BERTRAND
Am I awake?—No: 'tis delusion all!
My wildest wishes never soar'd to this;
Fortune anticipates my plot: he loves her,
Loves just whom I would have him love—loves Julia!
Orlando, yes, I'll play thee at my will:
Poor puppet! thou hast trusted to my hand
The strings by which I'll move thee to thy ruin,
And make thee, too, the instrument of vengeance,
Of glorious vengeance, on the man I hate.

[Exit.

ACT II

Enter **JULIA** and **EMMELINA**

JULIA

How many cares perplex the maid who loves!
Cares which the vacant heart can never know.
You fondly tremble for a brother's life;
Orlando mourns the absence of a friend,
Guildford is anxious for a son's renown.
In my poor heart your various terrors meet,
With added fears and fonder apprehensions:
They all unite in me, I feel for all,—
His life, his fame, his absence, and his love:
For he may live to see his native home,
And he may live to bless a sister's hopes,
May live to gratify impatient friendship,
May live to crown a father's house with honour,
May live to glory, yet be dead to love.

EMMELINA

Forbear these fears; they wound my brother's honour:
Julia, a brave man must be ever faithful;
Cowards alone dare venture to be false;
Cowards alone dare injure trusting virtue,
And with bold perjuries affront high heaven.

JULIA

I know his faith, and venerate his virtues;
I know his heart is tender as 'tis brave:
That all his father's worth, his sister's softness,
Meet in his generous breast—and yet I fear——
Who ever lov'd like me, and did not fear?

[Enter **GUILDFORD**.

GUILFORD

Where are my friends, my daughter where is Julia?
How shall I speak the fulness of my heart?
My son, my Rivers, will this day return.

EMMELINA

My dearest brother!

JULIA

Ha! my Rivers comes!
Propitious heaven!

EMMELINA

And yet my Julia trembles.

JULIA

Have I not cause? my Rivers comes! but how?
I dread to ask, and yet I die to hear.
My lord—you know the terms——

GUILFORD
He comes a conqueror!
He comes as Guildford's son should ever come!
The battle's o'er, the English arms successful;
And Rivers, like an English warrior, hastes
To lay his laurels at the feet of beauty.

[Exit.

JULIA
My joy oppresses me!

EMMELINA
And see, Orlando!
How will the welcome news transport his soul,
And raise his drooping heart! With caution tell him,
Lest the o'erwhelming rapture be too much
For his dejected mind.

[Enter **ORLANDO** and **BERTRAND**.

JULIA
My Lord Orlando,
Wherefore that troubled air? No more you dwell
On your once darling theme; you speak no more
The praises of your Rivers: is he chang'd?
Is he not still the gallant friend you lov'd,
As virtuous and as valiant?

ORLANDO
Still the same;
He must be ever virtuous, ever valiant.

EMMELINA
If Rivers is the same, then must I think
Orlando greatly chang'd; you speak not of him,
Nor long for his return, as you were wont.
How did you use to spend the live-long day
In telling some new wonders of your friend,
Till night broke in upon the unfinish'd tale;
And when 'twas o'er, you would begin again,
And we again would listen with delight,
With fresh delight, as if we had not heard it!
Does Rivers less deserve, or you less love?

ORLANDO

Have I not lov'd him? was my friendship cold?
When any prais'd his glories in the field,
My raptur'd heart has bounded at the tale.
Me though I grew illustrious from his glory,
And rich from his renown: to hear him prais'd,
More proud than if I had achiev'd his deeds,
And reap'd myself the harvest of his fame.
How have I trembled for a life so dear,
When his too ardent soul, despising caution,
Has plung'd him in the foremost ranks of war,
As if in love with danger.

JULIA

Valiant Rivers!
How does thy greatness justify my love!

BERTRAND

He's distant far, so I may safely praise him. [Aside.
I claim some merit in my love of Rivers,
Since I admire the virtues that eclipse me:
With pleasure I survey those dazzling heights
My gay, inactive temper cannot reach.

EMMELINA

Spoke like my honest cousin. Then, Orlando,
Since such the love you bear your noble friend,
How will your heart sustain the mighty joy
The news I tell will give you? Yes, Orlando,
Restrain the transports of your grateful friendship,
And hear, with moderation, hear me tell you
That Rivers will return—

ORLANDO

How? when?

EMMELINA

This day.

ORLANDO

Impossible!

BERTRAND

Then all my schemes are air.   [Aside.

EMMELINA

To-day I shall embrace my valiant brother!

JULIA
You droop, my Lord: did you not hear her right?
She told you that your Rivers would return,
Would come to crown your friendship and our hopes.

ORLANDO
He is most welcome! Is he not my friend?
You say my Rivers comes.—Thy arm, good Bertrand.

BERTRAND
Joy to us all! joy to the Count Orlando!
Weak man, take care. [Aside to **ORLANDO**.

EMMELINA
My Lord! you are not well.

BERTRAND
Surprise and joy oppress him: I myself
Partake his transports. Rouse, my Lord, for shame.

EMMELINA
How is it with you now?

ORLANDO
Quite well—'tis past.

BERTRAND
The wonder's past, and nought but joy remains.

[Enter **GUILDFORD** and **RIVERS**.

GUILFORD
He's come! he's here! I have embrac'd my warrior;
Now take me, heaven; I have liv'd long enough.

JULIA
My Lord! my Rivers!

RIVERS
'Tis my Julia's self!
My life!

JULIA
My hero! Do I then behold thee?

RIVERS
Oh, my full heart! expect not words, my Julia!

EMMELINA
Rivers!

RIVERS
My sister! what an hour is this!
My own Orlando too!

ORLANDO
My noble friend!

RIVERS
This is such prodigality of bliss,
I scarce can think it real. Honest Bertrand,
Your hand; yours, my Orlando; yours, my father;
And, as a hand, I have a heart for all;
Love has enlarg'd it; from excess of love
I am become more capable of friendship.
My dearest Julia!

GUILFORD
She is thine, my son;
Thou hast deserv'd her nobly; thou hast won her,
Fulfill'd the terms—

RIVERS
Therefore I dare not ask her;
I would not claim my Julia as a debt,
But take her as a gift, and, oh, I swear
It is the dearest, richest, choicest gift.
The bounty of indulgent heaven could grant.

[**GUILDFORD** joins their hands.

JULIA
Spare me, my Lord.—As yet I scarce have seen you.
Confusion stops my tongue—yet I will own,
If there be truth or faith in woman's vows,
Then you have still been present to this heart,
And not a thought has wandered from its duty.

[Exeunt **JULIA** and **EMMELINA**.

RIVERS (looking after **JULIA**.)
Oh, generous Julia!

ORLANDO (aside to **BERTRAND**.)
Mark how much she loves him!

BERTRAND (aside to **ORLANDO.**)
Mere words, which the fond sex have always ready.

RIVERS
Forgive me, good Orlando, best of friends!
How my soul joys to meet thee on this shore!
Thus to embrace thee in my native England!

GUILFORD
England! the land of worth, the soil of heroes,
Where great Elizabeth the sceptre sways,
O'er a free, glorious, rich, and happy people!
Philosophy, not cloister'd up in schools,
The speculative dream of idle monks,
Attir'd in attic robe, here roams at large;
Wisdom is wealth, and science is renown.
Here sacred laws protect the meanest subject;
The bread that toil procures fair freedom sweetens;
And every peasant eats his homely meal,
Content and free, lord of his small domain.

RIVERS
Past are those Gothic days, and, thanks to heaven,
They are for ever pass'd, when English subjects
Were born the vassals of some tyrant lord!
When free-soul'd men were basely handed down
To the next heir, transmitted with their lands,
The shameful legacy from sire to son!

GUILFORD
But while thy generous soul, my noble boy,
Justly abhors oppression, yet revere
The plain stern virtues of our rough forefathers:
O never may the gallant sons of England
Lose their plain, manly, generous character;
Forego the glorious charter nature gave them,—
Beyond what kings can give, or laws bestow,—
Their candour, courage, constancy, and truth!

[Exeunt **GUILDFORD** and **RIVERS**.

ORLANDO
Stay, Bertrand, stay—Oh, pity my distraction!
This heart was never made to hide its feelings;
I had near betray'd myself.

BERTRAND

I trembled for you:
Remember that the eye of love is piercing,
And Emmelina mark'd you.

ORLANDO
'Tis too much!
My artless nature cannot bear disguise.
Think what I felt when unsuspecting Rivers
Press'd me with gen'rous rapture to his bosom,
Profess'd an honest joy, and call'd me friend!
I felt myself a traitor: yet I swear,
Yes, by that Power who sees the thoughts of men,
I swear, I love the gallant Rivers more
Than light or life! I love, but yet I fear, him:
I shrunk before the lustre of his virtue—
I felt as I had wrong'd him—felt abash'd.
I cannot bear this conflict in my soul,
And therefore have resolv'd—

BERTRAND
On what?

ORLANDO
To fly.

BERTRAND
To fly from Julia?

ORLANDO
Yes, to fly from all,
From every thing I love; to fly from Rivers,
From Emmelina, from myself, from thee:
From Julia? no—that were impossible,
For I shall bear her image in my soul;
It is a part of me, the dearest part;
So closely interwoven with my being,
That I can never lose the dear remembrance,
'Till I am robb'd of life and her together.

BERTRAND
'Tis cowardice to fly.

ORLANDO
'Tis death to stay.

BERTRAND
Where would you go?—How lost in thought he stands!   [Aside.
A vulgar villain now would use persuasion,

And by his very earnestness betray
The thing he meant to hide: I'll coolly wait,
Till the occasion shows me how to act;
Then turn it to my purpose.—Ho! Orlando!
Where would you go?

ORLANDO
To solitude, to hopeless banishment!
Yes, I will shroud my youth in those dark cells
Where Disappointment steals Devotion's name,
To cheat the wretched votary into ruin;
There will I live in love with misery:
Ne'er shall the sight of mirth profane my grief;
The sound of joy shall never charm my ear,
Nor music reach it, save when the slow bell
Wakes the dull brotherhood to lifeless prayer.
Then, when the slow-retreating world recedes,
When warm desires are cold, and passion dead,
And all things but my Julia are forgotten,
One thought of her shall fire my languid soul,
Chase the faint orison, and feed despair.

BERTRAND
What! with monastic, lazy drones retire,
And chant cold hymns with holy hypocrites?
First perish all the sex! Forbid it, manhood!
Where is your nobler self? For shame, Orlando;
Renounce this superstitious, whining weakness,
Or I shall blush to think I call'd you friend.

ORLANDO
What can I do?

BERTRAND (after a pause.)
Beg she'll defer the marriage
But for one single day; do this, and leave
The rest to me: she shall be thine.

ORLANDO
How say'st thou?
What, wrong her virtue?

BERTRAND
Still this cant of virtue!
This pomp of words, this phrase without a meaning!
I grant that honour's something, manly honour;
I'd fight, I'd burn, I'd bleed, I'd die for honour:
But what's this virtue?

ORLANDO

Ask you what it is?
Why 'tis what libertines themselves adore;
'Tis that which wakens love and kindles rapture
Beyond the rosy lip or starry eye.
Virtue! 'tis that which gives a secret force
To common charms; but to true loveliness
Lends colouring celestial. Such its power,
That she who ministers to guilty pleasures,
Assumes its semblance when she most would please.
Virtue! 'tis that ethereal energy
Which gives to body spirit, soul to beauty.

[Exit.

BERTRAND

Curse on his principles! Yet I shall shake them;
Yes, I will bend his spirit to my will,
Now while 'tis warm with passion, and will take
Whatever mould my forming hand will give it.
'Tis worthy of my genius! Then I love
This Emmelina—true she loves not me—
But should young Rivers die, his father's lands
Would all be mine.—Is Rivers then immortal?
Come—Guildford's lands, and his proud daughter's hand
Are worth some thought.—Aid me, ye spurs to genius!
Love, mischief, poverty, revenge, and envy!

[Exit **BERTRAND**.

[Enter **EMMELINA** and **RIVERS** talking.

EMMELINA

Yet do not blame Orlando, good my brother;
He's still the same, that brave frank heart you lov'd;
Only his temper's chang'd, he is grown sad;
But that's no fault, I only am to blame;
Fond foolish heart, to give itself away
To one who gave me nothing in return!

RIVERS

How's this? my father said Orlando lov'd thee.

EMMELINA

Indeed I thought so—he was kinder once;
Nay still he loves, or my poor heart deceives me.

RIVERS

If he has wrong'd thee—yet I know he could not;
His gallant soul is all made up of virtues,
And I would rather doubt myself than him.
Yet tell me all the story of your loves,
And let a brother's fondness soothe thy cares.

EMMELINA

When to this castle first Orlando came,
A welcome guest to all, to me most welcome;
Yes, spite of maiden shame and burning blushes,
Let me confess he was most welcome to me.
At first my foolish heart so much deceiv'd me,
I thought I lov'd him for my brother's sake;
But when I closely search'd this bosom traitor,
I found, alas! I lov'd him for his own.

RIVERS

Blush not to own it; 'twas a well-plac'd flame!
I glory in the merit of my friend,
And love my sister more for loving him.

EMMELINA

He talk'd of you; I listen'd with delight,
And fancied 'twas the subject only charm'd me;
But when Orlando chose another theme,
Forgive me, Rivers, but I listen'd still
With undiminish'd joy—he talk'd of love,
Nor was that theme less grateful than the former.
I seem'd the very idol of his soul;
Rivers, he said, would thank me for the friendship
I bore to his Orlando; I believ'd him.
Julia was absent then—but what of Julia?

RIVERS

Aye, what of her, indeed? why nam'd you Julia?
You could not surely think?—no, that were wild.
Why did you mention Julia?

EMMELINA (confusedly)

Nay, 'twas nothing,
'Twas accident, nor had my words a meaning;
If I did name her—'twas to note the time—
To mark the period of Orlando's coldness—
The circumstance was casual, and but meant
To date the change; it aim'd at nothing further.

RIVERS (agitated.)

'Tis very like—no more—I'm satisfied—
You talk as I had doubts: what doubts have I?
Why do you labour to destroy suspicions
Which never had a birth? Is she not mine?
Mine by the fondest ties of dear affection?—
But did Orlando change at her return?
Did he grow cold? It could not be for that;
You may mistake.—And yet you said 'twas then;
Was it precisely then—I only ask
For the fond love I bear my dearest sister.

EMMELINA
'Twas as I said.

RIVERS (recovering himself.)
He loves thee, Emmelina:
These starts of passion, this unquiet temper,
Betray how much he loves thee: yes, my sister,
He fears to lose thee, fears his father's will
May dash his rising hopes, nor give thee to him.

EMMELINA
Oh, flatterer! thus to soothe my easy nature
With tales of possible, unlikely bliss!
Because it may be true, my credulous heart
Whispers it is, and fondly loves to cherish
The feeble glimmering of a sickly hope.

RIVERS
This precious moment, worth a tedious age
Of vulgar time, I've stol'n from love and Julia;
She waits my coming, and a longer stay
Were treason to her beauty and my love.
Doubts vanish, fears recede, and fondness triumphs.

[Exeunt.

ACT III

SCENE—A Garden

EMMELINA
Why do my feet unbidden seek this grove?
Why do I trace his steps? I thought him here;
This is his hour of walking, and these shades

His daily haunt: oft have they heard his vows:
Ah! fatal vows, which stole my peace away!
But now he shuns my presence: yet who knows,
He may not be ungrateful, but unhappy!
Yes he will come to clear his past offences,
With such prevailing eloquence will plead,
So mourn his former faults, so blame his coldness,
And by ten thousand graceful ways repair them,
That I shall think I never was offended.
He comes, and every doubt's at once dispell'd:
'Twas fancy all; he never meant to wrong me.

[Enter **ORLANDO.**

ORLANDO
Why, at this hour of universal joy,
When every heart beats high with grateful rapture,
And pleasure dances her enchanting round,
O tell me why, at this auspicious hour,
You quit the joyful circle of your friends,
Rob social pleasure of its sweetest charm,
And leave a void e'en in the happiest hearts,
An aching void which only you can fill?
Why do you seek these unfrequented shades?
Why court these gloomy haunts unfit for beauty;
But made for meditation and misfortune?

EMMELINA
I might retort the charge, my lord Orlando!
I might enquire how the lov'd friend of Rivers,
Whom he has held deep-rooted in his heart,
Beyond a brother's dearness, sav'd his life,
And cherish'd it, when sav'd, beyond his own;—
I might enquire, why, when this Rivers comes,
After long tedious months of expectation,
Alive, victorious, and as firm in friendship
As fondness could have wish'd or fancy feign'd;
I might enquire why thus Orlando shuns him—
Why thus he courts this melancholy gloom,
As if he were at variance with delight,
And scorn'd to mingle in the general joy?

ORLANDO
Oh, my fair monitress! I have deserv'd
Your gentle censure. Henceforth I'll be gay.

EMMELINA
Julia complains, too, of you.

ORLANDO
Ah! does Julia?
If Julia chides me, I have err'd indeed;
For harshness is a stranger to her nature.
But why does she complain? O tell me wherefore?
That I may soon repair the unwilling crime,
And prove my heart at least ne'er meant to wrong her.

EMMELINA
Why so alarm'd?

ORLANDO
Alarm'd!

EMMELINA
Indeed you seem'd so.

ORLANDO
Sure you mistake. Alarm'd! oh, no, I was not;
There was no cause—I could not be alarm'd
Upon so slight a ground. Something you said,
But what I know not, of your friend.

EMMELINA
Of Julia?

ORLANDO
That Julia was displeas'd—was it not so?
'Twas that, or something like it.

EMMELINA
She complains
That you avoid her.

ORLANDO
How! that I avoid her?
Did Julia say so? ah! you have forgot—
It could not be.

EMMELINA
Why are you terrified?

ORLANDO
No,
Not terrified—I am not—but were those
Her very words? you might mistake her meaning;
Did Julia say Orlando shunn'd her presence?

Oh! did she, could she say so?

EMMELINA
If she did,
Why this disorder? there's no cause.

ORLANDO
No cause?
O there's a cause of dearer worth than empire!
Quick let me fly, and find the fair upbraider;
Tell her she wrongs me, tell her I would die
Rather than meet her anger.

[**EMMELINA** faints.

Ah, she faints!
What have I said? curse my imprudent tongue!
Look up, sweet innocence! my Emmelina—
My gentle friend, awake! look up, fair creature!
'Tis your Orlando calls.

EMMELINA
Orlando's voice!
Methought he talk'd of love—nay, do not mock me;
My heart is but a weak, a very weak one!
I am not well—perhaps I've been to blame.
Spare my distress: the error has been mine.

[Exit **EMMELINA**.

ORLANDO
So then, all's over; I've betray'd my secret,
And stuck a poison'd dagger in her heart,
Her innocent heart. Why, what a wretch am I!
Ruin approaches;—shall I tamely meet it,
And dally with destruction till it blast me?
No, I will fly thee, Julia, fly for ever.
Ah, fly! what then becomes of Emmelina?
Shall I abandon her? it must be so;
Better escape with this poor wreck of honour,
Than hazard all by staying—Rivers here?

[Enter **RIVERS**.

RIVERS
The same. My other self! My own Orlando!
I came to seek thee; 'twas in thy kind bosom
My suffering soul repos'd its secret cares,

When doubts and difficulties stood before me;
And now, now, when my prosperous fortune shines,
And gilds the smiling hour with her bright beams,
Shall I become a niggard of my bliss,
Defraud thee of thy portion of my joys,
And rob thee of thy well-earn'd claim to share them?

ORLANDO
That I have ever lov'd thee, witness Heaven!
That I have thought thy friendship the best blessing
That mark'd the fortune of my happier days,
I here attest the sovereign Judge of hearts!
Then think, O think, what anguish I endure,
When I declare, in bitterness of spirit,
That we must part—

RIVERS
What does Orlando mean?

ORLANDO
That I must leave thee, Rivers; must renounce
Thy lov'd society.

RIVERS
Thou hast been injur'd;
Thy merit has been slighted; sure my father,
Who knew how dear I held thee, would not wrong thee.

ORLANDO
He is all goodness; no—there is a cause—
Seek not to know it.

RIVERS
Now, by holy friendship!
I swear thou shalt not leave me; what! just now,
When I have safely pass'd so many perils,
Escap'd so many deaths, return'd once more
To the kind arms of long-desiring friendship;
Just now, when I expected such a welcome,
As happy souls in Paradise bestow
Upon a new inhabitant, who comes
To taste their blessedness, you coldly tell me
You will depart; it must not be, Orlando.

ORLANDO
It must, it must.

RIVERS

Ah, must! then tell me wherefore?

ORLANDO
I would not dim thy dawn of happiness,
Nor shade the brighter beams of thy good fortune,
With the dark sullen cloud that hangs o'er mine.

RIVERS
Is this the heart of him I call'd my friend,
Full of the graceful weakness of affection?
How have I known it bend at my request!
How lose the power of obstinate resistance,
Because his friend entreated! This Orlando!
How is he chang'd!

ORLANDO
Alas, how chang'd indeed!
How dead to every relish of delight!
How chang'd in all but in his love for thee!
Yet think not that my nature is grown harder,
That I have lost that ductile, yielding heart;
Rivers, I have not—oh! 'tis still too soft;
E'en now it melts, it bleeds in tenderness—
Farewell!—I dare not trust myself—farewell!

RIVERS
Then thou resolv'st to go?

ORLANDO
This very day.

RIVERS
What do I hear? To-day! It must not be:
This is the day that makes my Julia mine.

ORLANDO
Wed her to-day?

RIVERS
This day unites me to her;
Then stay at least till thou behold'st her mine.

ORLANDO
Impossible! another day were ruin.

RIVERS
Then let me fly to Julia, and conjure her
To bless me with her hand this hour—this moment.

ORLANDO
Oh, no, no, no.

RIVERS
I will: in such a cause
Surely she will forego the rigid forms
Of cold decorum; then, my best Orlando!
I shall receive my Julia from thy hand;
The blessing will be doubled! I shall owe
The precious gift of love to sacred friendship!

ORLANDO
Canst thou bear this, my heart?

RIVERS
Then, my Orlando,
Since thy unkind reserve denies my heart
Its partnership in this thy hoard of sorrows,
I will not press to know it: thou shalt go
Soon as the holy priest has made us one;
For, oh! 'twill soothe thee in the hour of parting,
To know I'm in possession of my love,
To think I'm blest with Julia, to reflect
Thou gav'st her to my arms, my bride! my wife!

ORLANDO
Ah! my brain turns!

RIVERS
'Tis as I thought; I'll try him.   [Aside.
Now answer me, Orlando, and with truth;
Hide nothing from thy friend—dost thou not love?

ORLANDO
Ha! how? I am betray'd! he reads my heart.

RIVERS
Hast thou, with all that tenderness of soul,
From love's infection kept thy yielding heart?
Say, could'st thou bask in all the blaze of beauty,
And never feel its warmth?—Impossible!
Oh! I shall probe thy soul till thou confess
The conquering fair one's name—but why confess?
Come, come, I know full well—

ORLANDO
Ha! dost thou know?

And knowing, dost thou suffer me to live?
And dost thou know my guilt, and call me friend?
He mocks but to destroy me!

RIVERS
Come, no more;
Love is a proud, an arbitrary god,
And will not choose as rigid fathers bid;
I know that thine has destin'd for thy bride
A Tuscan maid; but hearts disdain all force.

ORLANDO
How's this? what! dost thou justify my passion?

RIVERS
Applaud it—glory in it—will assist it.
She is so fair, so worthy to be lov'd,
That I should be thy rival, were not she
My sister.

ORLANDO
How!

RIVERS
She is another Julia.

ORLANDO
I stood upon a fearful precipice—
I'm giddy still—oh, yes! I understand thee—
Thy beauteous sister! what a wretch I've been!
Oh, Rivers! too much softness has undone me.
Yet I will never wrong the maid I love,
Nor injure thee; first, let Orlando perish!

RIVERS
Be more explicit.

ORLANDO
For the present spare me.
Think not too hardly of me, noble Rivers!
I am a man, and full of human frailties;
But hate like hell the crime which tempts me on.
When I am ready to depart, I'll see thee,
Clear all my long accounts of love and honour,
Remove thy doubts, embrace thee, and expire.

[Exit **ORLANDO**.

RIVERS
It must be so—to what excess he loves her!
Yet wherefore not demand her? for his birth
May claim alliance with the proudest fortune.
Sure there's some hidden cause—perhaps—ah, no!
Turn from that thought, my soul! 'twas vile suspicion;
And I could hate the heart which but conceiv'd it.
'Tis true their faith is different—then his father,
Austere and rigid, dooms him to another.
That must not be—these bars shall be remov'd;
I'll serve him with my life, nor taste of bliss,
'Till I have sought to bless the friend I love.

[Exit.

[Re-enter **ORLANDO**.

ORLANDO
Wed her to-day? wed her perhaps this hour?
Hasten the rites for me? I give her to him?
I stand a tame spectator of their bliss?
I live a patient witness of their joy?
First let this dagger drink my heart's warm blood.

[Takes a dagger from his bosom, then sees **JULIA**.

The sorceress comes! oh, there's a charm about her
Which holds my hand, and makes me wish to live.
I shudder at her sight! open, thou earth,
And save me from the peril of her charms!

[Puts up the dagger.

[Enter **JULIA**.

JULIA
Methought I heard the cry of one in pain;
From hence it came; ah, me! my lord Orlando!
What means that sigh? that agonising voice?
Those groans which rend your heart? those frantic looks?
Indeed I'm terrified. What would you do?

ORLANDO (furiously)
Die!

JULIA
Talk you of death? renounce the fatal thought;
Live for my sake, Orlando.

ORLANDO
For thy sake?
That were indeed a cause to live for ages,
Would nature but extend the narrow limits
Of human life so far.

JULIA
And for the sake
Of Rivers; live for both; he sends me here
To beg you would delay your purpos'd parting;
His happiness, he swears, if you are absent
Will be but half complete.

ORLANDO
Is it to-night?
This marriage, Julia, did you say to-night?

JULIA
It is, and yet you leave us.

ORLANDO
No—I'll stay,
Since you command, stay and expire before you.

JULIA
What mean you?

ORLANDO
That I'll perish at the feet
Of—Rivers.

JULIA
Tell your sorrows to my lord;
Upon his faithful breast repose the weight
That presses you to earth.

ORLANDO
Tell him? Tell Rivers?
Is he not yours? Does not the priest now wait
To make you one? Then do not mock me thus:
What leisure can a happy bridegroom find
To think upon so lost a wretch as I am?
You hate me, Julia.

JULIA
Hate you? how you wrong me!
Live to partake our joy.

ORLANDO
Hope you for joy?

JULIA
Have I not cause? Am I not lov'd by Rivers?
Rivers, the best, the bravest of his sex!
Whose valour fabled heroes ne'er surpass'd,
Whose virtues teach the young and charm the old;
Whose graces are the wonder of our sex,
And envy of his own!

ORLANDO
Enough! enough!
O spare this prodigality of praise.
But, Julia, if you would not here behold me
Stretch'd at your feet a lifeless bloody corpse,
Promise what I shall now request.

JULIA
What is it?

ORLANDO
That till to-morrow's sun, I ask no longer,
You will defer this marriage.

JULIA
Ah! defer it?
Impossible; what would my Rivers think?

ORLANDO
No matter what; 'tis for his sake I ask it:
His peace, his happiness, perhaps his life
Depends on what I ask.

JULIA
His life? the life of Rivers?
Some dreadful thought seems lab'ring in your breast;
Explain this horrid mystery.

ORLANDO
I dare not.
If you comply, before to-morrow's dawn
All will be well, the danger past; then finish
These—happy nuptials; but if you refuse,
Tremble for him you love; the altar's self
Will be no safeguard from a madman's rage.

JULIA
What rage? what madman? what remorseless villain?
Orlando—will not you protect your friend?
Think how he loves you—he would die for you—
Then save him, on my knees, I beg you save him—

[Kneels.

Oh! guard my Rivers from this bloody foe.

ORLANDO
Dearer than life I love him—ask no more,
But promise, in the awful face of Heaven,
To do what I request—and promise, further,
Not to disclose the cause.

JULIA
Oh, save him! save him!

ORLANDO
'Tis to preserve him that I ask it: promise,
Or see me fall before you.
[He draws the dagger, she still kneeling.

JULIA
I do promise.
Hide, hide that deadly weapon—I do promise.

[Rises.

How wild you look! you tremble more than I.
I'll call my Rivers hither.

ORLANDO
Not for worlds.
If you have mercy in your nature, Julia,
Retire. Oh, leave me quickly to myself;
Do not expose me to the strong temptation
Which now assaults me.—Yet you are not gone.

JULIA
Be more compos'd; I leave you with regret.
(As she goes out.) His noble mind is shaken from its seat!
What may these transports mean? Heav'n guard my Rivers!

[As **JULIA** goes out, enter **BERTRAND**; he speaks behind.)

BERTRAND

Why, this is well; this has a face; she weeps,
He seems disordered.—Now to learn the cause,
And then make use of what I hear by chance,
As of a thing I knew.

[He listens.

ORLANDO (after a pause.)
And is she gone?
Her parting words shot fire into my soul;
Did she not say she left me with regret?
Her look was tender, and the starting tear
Fill'd her bright eye; she left me with regret—
She own'd it too.

BERTRAND
'Twill do.
(Comes forward.) What have you done?
The charming Julia is dissolv'd in woe,
Her radiant eyes are quench'd in floods of tears;
For you they fall; her blushes have confess'd it.

ORLANDO
For me? what say'st thou? Julia weep for me!
Yet she is gentle, and she would have wept
For thee; for any who but seem'd unhappy.

BERTRAND
Ungrateful!

ORLANDO
How?

BERTRAND
Not by her tears, I judge,
But by her words not meant for me to hear.

ORLANDO
What did she say? What didst thou hear, good Bertrand?
Speak—I'm on fire.

BERTRAND
It is not safe to tell you.
Farewell! I would not injure Rivers.

ORLANDO
Stay,
Or tell me all, or I renounce thy friendship.

BERTRAND

That threat unlocks my tongue; I must not lose thee.
Sweet Julia wept, clasp'd her fair hands, and cried,
Why was I left a legacy to Rivers,
Robb'd of the power of choice? Seeing me she started,
Would have recall'd her words, blush'd, and retir'd.

ORLANDO

No more; thou shalt not tempt me to my ruin;
Deny what thou hast said, deny it quickly,
Ere I am quite undone; for, oh! I feel
Retreating virtue touches its last post,
And my lost soul now verges on destruction.
—Bertrand, she promis'd to defer the marriage.

BERTRAND

Then my point's gain'd; that will make Rivers jealous. [Aside.
She loves you.

ORLANDO

No; and even if she did,
I have no hope.

BERTRAND

You are too scrupulous.
Be bold and be successful; sure of this,
There is no crime a woman sooner pardons
Than that of which her beauty is the cause.

ORLANDO

Shall I defraud my friend? he bled to gain her!
What! rob the dear preserver of my life
Of all that makes the happiness of his?
And yet her beauty might excuse a falsehood;
Nay, almost sanctify a perjury.
Perdition's in that thought—'twas born in hell.
My soul is up in arms, my reason's lost,
And love, and rage, and jealousy, and honour,
Pull my divided heart, and tear my soul.   [Exit.

BERTRAND

Rave on, and beat thy wings; poor bird! thou'rt lim'd,
And vain will be thy struggles to get loose.
—How much your very honest men lack prudence!
Though all the nobler virtues fill one scale,
Yet place but Indiscretion in the other;
In worldly business, and the ways of men,

That single folly weighs the balance down,
While all th' ascending virtues kick the beam.
Here's this Orlando now, of rarest parts,
Honest, heroic, generous, frank, and kind
As inexperience of the world can make him;
Yet shall this single weakness, this imprudence,
Pull down unheard-of plagues upon his head,
And snare his heedless soul beyond redemption:
While dull unfeeling hearts, and frozen spirits,
Sordidly safe, secure, because untempted,
Look up and wonder at the generous crime
They wanted wit to frame, and souls to dare.

ACT IV

SCENE—An Apartment

EMMELINA
How many ways there are of being wretched!
The avenues to happiness how few!
When will this busy, fluttering heart be still?
When will it cease to feel and beat no more?
E'en now it shudders with a dire presage
Of something terrible it fears to know.
Ent'ring, I saw my venerable father
In earnest conference with the Count Orlando;
Shame and confusion fill'd Orlando's eye,
While stern resentment flush'd my father's cheek.
And look, he comes with terror on his brow!
But, oh! he sees me, sees his child; and now
The terror of his look is lost in love,
In fond, paternal love.

[Enter **GUILDFORD**.

GUILFORD
Come to my arms,
And there conceal that penetrating eye,
Lest it should read what I would hide for ever,
Would hide from all, but most would hide from thee—
Thy father's grief, his shame, his rage, his tears.

EMMELINA
Tears! heaven and earth! see if he does not weep!

GUILFORD

He who has drawn this sorrow from my eyes
Shall pay me back again in tears of blood.
'Tis for thy sake I weep.

EMMELINA
Ah, weep for me?
Hear, Heaven, and judge; hear, Heaven, and punish me!
If any crime of mine—

GUILFORD
Thou art all innocence;
Just what a parent's fondest wish would frame;
No fault of thine e'er stain'd thy father's cheek;
For if I blush'd, it was to hear thy virtues,
And think that thou wast mine: and if I wept,
It was from joy and gratitude to heaven,
That made me father of a child like thee.
Orlando—

EMMELINA
What of him?

GUILFORD
I cannot tell thee;
An honest shame, a virtuous pride forbids.

EMMELINA
Oh, speak!

GUILFORD
Canst thou not guess, and spare thy father?

EMMELINA
'Tis possible I can—and yet I will not:
Tell me the worst while I have sense to hear.
Thou wilt not speak—nay, never turn away;
Dost thou not know that fear is worse than grief?
There may be bounds to grief, fear knows no bounds:
In grief we know the worst of what we feel,
But who can tell the end of what we fear?
Grief mourns some sorrow palpable and known,
But fear runs wild with horrible conjecture.

GUILFORD
Then hear the worst, and arm thy soul to bear it.
My child!—he has—Orlando has refus'd thee.

EMMELINA (after a long pause.)

'Tis well—'tis very well—'tis as it should be.

GUILFORD
Oh, there's an eloquence in that mute woe
Which mocks all language. Speak, relieve thy heart,
Thy bursting heart; thy father cannot bear it.
Am I a man? no more of this, fond eyes!
I am grown weaker than a chidden infant,
While not a sigh escapes to tell thy pain.

EMMELINA
See, I am calm; I do not shed a tear;
The warrior weeps, the woman is a hero!

GUILFORD (embraces her.)
My glorious child! now thou art mine, indeed!
Forgive me if I thought thee fond and weak.
I have a Roman matron for my daughter,
And not a feeble girl. And yet I fear,
For, oh! I know thy tenderness of soul;
I fear this silent anguish but portends
Some dread convulsion soon to burst in horrors.

EMMELINA
I will not shame thy blood; and yet, my father,
Methinks thy daughter should not be refus'd!
Refus'd? It has a harsh, ungrateful sound;
Thou shouldst have found a softer term of scorn.
And have I then been held so cheap? Refus'd?
Been treated like the light ones of my sex,
Held up to sale? been offer'd, and refus'd?

GUILFORD
Long have I known thy love; I thought it mutual:
I met him—talk'd of marriage—

EMMELINA
Ah! no more:
I am rejected;—does not that suffice?
Excuse my pride the mortifying tale;
Spare me particulars of how and when,
And do not parcel out thy daughter's shame.
No flowers of rhetoric can change the fact,
No arts of speech can varnish o'er my shame:
Orlando has refus'd me!

GUILFORD
Villain! villain!

He shall repent this outrage.

EMMELINA
Think no more on't:
I'll teach thee how to bear it; I'll grow proud,
As gentle spirits still are apt to do
When cruel slight or killing scorn assails them.
Come, virgin dignity; come, female pride;
Come, wounded modesty; come, slighted love;
Come, conscious worth; come, too, O black despair!
Support me, arm me, fill me with my wrongs!
Sustain this feeble spirit!—Yes, my father,
But for thy share in this sad tale of shame,
I think I could have borne it.

GUILFORD
Thou hast a brother;
He shall assert thy cause.

EMMELINA
First strike me dead!
No, in the wild distraction of my spirit,
In this dread conflict of my breaking heart,
Hear my fond pleading—save me from that curse;
Thus I adjure thee by the dearest ties   [Kneels.
Which link society; by the sweet names
Of parent and of child; by all the joys
These tender claims have yielded, I adjure thee
Breathe not this fatal secret to my brother;
Let him not know his sister was refus'd!
Spare me that exquisite, that perfect ruin!
Conceive the mighty woe I cannot speak,
And tremble to become a childless father.

[Exit **EMMELINA**.

GUILFORD
What art thou, Life? thou lying vanity!
Thou promiser, who never meanst to pay!
This beating storm will crush my feeble age!
Yet let me not complain; I have a son,
Just such a son as Heaven in mercy gives,
When it would bless supremely: he is happy;
His ardent wishes will this day be crown'd;
He weds the maid he loves: in him, at least,
My soul will yet taste comfort.—See; he's here;
He seems disorder'd.

[Enter **RIVERS** but not seeing **GUILDFORD**.

RIVERS
Yes, I fondly thought
Not all the tales which malice might devise,
Not all the leagues combined hell might form,
Could shake her steady soul.

GUILDFORD
What means my son?
Where is thy bride?

RIVERS
O name her not!

GUILDFORD
Not name her?

RIVERS
No; if possible, not think of her;
Would I could help it:—Julia! oh, my Julia!
Curse my fond tongue! I said I would not name her:
I did not think to do it, but my heart
Is full of her idea; her lov'd image
So fills my soul, it shuts out other thoughts;
My lips resolving not to frame the sound,
Dwell on her name, and all my talk is Julia!

GUILDFORD
'Tis as it should be; ere the midnight bell
Sound in thy raptur'd ear, this charming Julia
Will be thy wife.

RIVERS
No.

GUILDFORD
How?

RIVERS
She has refus'd.

GUILDFORD
Say'st thou?

RIVERS
She has.

GUILFORD

Why, who would be a father!
Who that could guess the wretchedness it brings,
But would entreat of Heaven to write him childless!

RIVERS

'Twas but a little hour ago we parted,
As happy lovers should; but when again
I sought her presence, with impatient haste,
Told her the priest, the altar, all was ready;
She blush'd, she wept, and vow'd it could not be;
That reasons of importance to our peace
Forbad the nuptial rites to be perform'd
Before to-morrow.

GUILFORD

She consents to-morrow!
She but defers the marriage, not declines it.

RIVERS

Mere subterfuge! mere female artifice!
What reason should forbid our instant union?
Wherefore to-morrow? wherefore not to-night?
What difference could a few short hours have made?
Or if they could, why not avow the cause?

GUILFORD

I have grown old in camps, have liv'd in courts;
The toils of bright ambition have I known,
Woo'd greatness and enjoy'd it, till disgust
Follow'd possession; still I fondly look'd
Through the false perspective for distant joy;
Hop'd for the hour of honourable ease,
When, safe from all the storms and wrecks of fate,
My shatter'd bark at rest, I might enjoy
An old man's blessings, liberty and leisure,
Domestic happiness, and smiling peace.
The hour of age, indeed, is come! I feel it:
Feel it in all its sorrows, pains, and cares;
But where, oh, where's th' untasted peace it promis'd?

[Exit **GUILDFORD**.

RIVERS

I would not deeper wound my father's peace;
But I would hide the cause of my resentment,
Till all be known; and yet I know too much.
It must be so—his grief, his sudden parting:

Fool that I was, not to perceive at once—
But friendship blinded me, and love betray'd.
Bertrand was right, he told me she was chang'd,
And would, on some pretence, delay the marriage.
I hop'd 'twas malice all.—Yonder she comes,
Dissolv'd in tears; I cannot see them fall,
And be a man; I will not, dare not meet her;
Her blandishments would soothe me to false peace,
And if she ask'd it, I should pardon all.   [Exit.

[Enter **JULIA**.

JULIA
Stay, Rivers! stay, barbarian! hear me speak!
Return, inhuman!—best belov'd, return:
Oh! I will tell thee all, restore thy peace,
Kneel at thy feet, and sue for thy forgiveness.
He hears me not—alas! he will not hear.
Break, thou poor heart, since Rivers is unkind.

[Enter **ORLANDO**.

ORLANDO
Julia in tears!

JULIA
Alas! you have undone me!
Behold the wretched victim of her promise!
I urg'd, at your request, the fatal suit
Which has destroy'd my peace; Rivers suspects me,
And I am wretched!

ORLANDO
Better 'tis to weep
A temporary ill than weep for ever;
That anguish must be mine.

JULIA
Ha! weep for ever!
Can they know wretchedness who know not love?

ORLANDO
Not love! oh, cruel friendship! tyrant honour!

JULIA
Friendship! alas, how cold art thou to love!

ORLANDO

Too well I know it; both alike destroy me,
I am the slave of both, and more than either
The slave of honour.

JULIA
If you then have felt
The bitter agonies—

ORLANDO
Talk you of agonies?
You who are lov'd again! No! they are mine;
Mine are the agonies of hopeless passion;
Yes, I do love—I dote, I die for love!

[He falls at her feet.

Julia!

JULIA
What dost thou mean? Unfold this fatal secret.

ORLANDO
Nay, never start—I know I am a villain!
I know thy hand is destin'd to another,
That other, too, my friend, that friend the man
To whom I owe my life! Yes, I adore thee;
Spite of the black ingratitude, adore thee;
I dote upon my friend and yet betray him;
I'm bound to Emmelina, yet forsake her;
I honour virtue while I follow guilt;
I love the noble Rivers more than life,
But Julia more than honour.

JULIA
Hold! astonishment
Has seal'd my lips; whence sprung this monstrous daring?

ORLANDO (rises.)
From despair.

JULIA
What can you hope from me?

ORLANDO
Hope! nothing.
I would not aught receive, aught hope, but death.
Think'st thou I need reproach? think'st thou I need
To be reminded that my love's a crime?

That every moral tie forbids my passion?
But though I know that heav'n has plagues in store,
Yet mark—I do not, will not, can't repent;
I do not even wish to love thee less;
I glory in my crime: pernicious beauty!
Come, triumph in thy power, complete my woes;
Insult me with the praises of my rival,
The man on earth—whom most I ought to love!

JULIA
I leave thee to remorse, and to that penitence
Thy crime demands.

[Going.

ORLANDO
A moment stay.

JULIA
I dare not.

ORLANDO
Hear all my rival's worth, and all my guilt.
The unsuspecting Rivers sent me to thee,
To plead his cause; I basely broke my trust,
And, like a villain, pleaded for myself.

JULIA
Did he? Did Rivers? Then he loves me still—
Quick let me seek him out.

ORLANDO (takes out the dagger.)
First take this dagger;
Had you not forc'd it from my hand to-day,
I had not liv'd to know this guilty moment:
Take it, present it to the happy Rivers,
Tell him to plunge it in a traitor's heart,
Tell him his friend, Orlando, is that traitor,
Tell him Orlando forg'd the guilty tale,
Tell him Orlando was the only foe
Who at the altar would have murder'd Rivers,
And then have died himself.

JULIA
Farewell—repent—think better.

[Exit **JULIA.**

[As she goes out, he still looks after her.

[Enter **RIVERS**.

RIVERS
Turn, villain, turn!

ORLANDO
Ha! Rivers here?

RIVERS
Yes, Rivers.

ORLANDO
Gape wide, thou friendly earth, for ever hide me!
Rise, Alps, ye crashing mountains, bury me!

RIVERS
Nay, turn, look on me.

ORLANDO
Rivers! oh, I cannot,
I dare not, I have wrong'd thee.

RIVERS
Doubly wrong'd me;
Thy complicated crimes cry out for vengeance.

ORLANDO
Take it.

RIVERS
But I would take it as a man.
Draw.

[**RIVERS** draws.

ORLANDO
Not for a thousand worlds.

RIVERS
Not fight?
Why, thou'rt a coward, too, as well as villain:
I shall despise as well as hate thee.

ORLANDO
Do;
Yet wrong me not, for if I am a coward

'Tis but to thee: there does not breathe the man,
Thyself excepted, who durst call me so
And live; but, oh! 'tis sure to heaven and thee,
I am the veriest coward guilt e'er made.
Now, as thou art a man, revenge thyself:
Strike!

RIVERS
No, not stab thee like a base assassin,
But meet thee as a foe.

ORLANDO
Think of my wrongs.

RIVERS
I feel them here.

ORLANDO
Think of my treachery.

RIVERS
Oh, wherefore wast thou false? how have I lov'd thee!

ORLANDO
Of that no more: think of thy father's grief,
Of Emmelina's wrongs—

RIVERS
Provoke me not.

ORLANDO
Of Julia—

RIVERS
Ha! I shall forget my honour,
And do a brutal violence upon thee,
Would tarnish my fair fame. Villain and coward!
Traitor! will nothing rouse thee?

ORLANDO (drawing.)
Swelling heart!
Yet this I have deserv'd, all this, and more.

As they prepare to fight, enter **EMMELINA** hastily.

EMMELINA
Lend me your swiftness, lightnings—'tis too late.
See they're engag'd—oh, no—they live, both live!

Hold, cruel men!

RIVERS
Unlucky! 'tis my sister.

EMMELINA
Ye men of blood! if yet you have not lost
All sense of human kindness, love, or pity;
If ever you were dear to one another;
If ever you desire or look for mercy
When in the wild extremity of anguish,
You supplicate that Judge who has declar'd
That vengeance is his own—oh, hear me now;
Hear a fond wretch, whom mis'ry has made bold;
Spare, spare each other's life—spare your own souls.

ORLANDO (to **RIVERS**.)
Thou shouldst have struck at once! O tardy hand!

EMMELINA
Does death want engines? is his power curtail'd?
Has fell disease forgotten to destroy?
Are there not pestilence and spotted plagues,
Devouring deluges, consuming fires,
Earthquakes, volcanoes, hurricanes, and famine,
That man must perish by the hand of man?
Nay, to complete the horror, friend by friend?

RIVERS
What! shall I then endure this outrage tamely?

EMMELINA
No. If you covet death; if you're in love
With slaughter and destruction—does not war
Invite you to her banner? Far and wide
Her dire dominion reaches.—There seek death.
There fall without a crime. There, where no hate,
No individual rage, no private wrong,
Arms man against his brother.—Not as here,
Where both are often murderers in the act;
In the foul purpose—always.

RIVERS
Is honour nothing?

EMMELINA
Honour! O yes, I know him. 'Tis a phantom;
A shadowy figure wanting bulk and life;

Who, having nothing solid in himself,
Wraps his thin form in Virtue's plunder'd robe,
And steals her title. Honour! 'tis the fiend
Who feeds on orphans' tears and widows' groans,
And slakes his impious thirst in brothers' blood.
Honour! why, 'tis the primal law of hell!
The grand device to people the dark realms
With noble spirits, who, but for this curst honour,
Had been at peace on earth, or bless'd in heaven.
With this false honour Christians have no commerce,
Religion disavows, and truth disowns it.

ORLANDO (throws away his sword.)
An angel speaks, and angels claim obedience.

RIVERS (to **ORLANDO**.)
This is the heart thou hast wrong'd.

EMMELINA (comes up to **ORLANDO**.)
I pity thee;
Calamity has taught me how to pity;
Before I knew distress, my heart was hard;
But now it melts at ev'ry touch of woe;
And wholesome sufferings bring it back to virtue.
Rivers, he once was good and just like thee:
Who shall be proud and think he stands secure,
If thy Orlando's false?

RIVERS
Think of his crime.

EMMELINA
Oh, think of his temptation! think 'twas Julia;
Thy heart could not resist her; how should his?
It is the very error of his friendship.
Your souls were fram'd so very much alike,
He could not choose but love whom Rivers lov'd.

ORLANDO
Think'st thou there is in death a pang like this?
Strike, my brave friend! be sudden and be silent!
Death, which is terrible to happy men,
To me will be a blessing: I have lost
All that could make life dear; I've lost my friend;
I've stabb'd the peace of mind of that fair creature;
I have surviv'd my honour: this is dying!
The mournful fondness of officious love
Will plant no thorns upon my dying pillow;

No precious tears embalm my memory,
But curses follow it.

EMMELINA
See, Rivers melts;
He pities thee.

ORLANDO
I'll spare thy noble heart
The pain of punishing: Orlando's self
Revenges both.

[Goes to stab himself with the dagger.

EMMELINA
Barbarian! kill me first.

RIVERS (snatching the dagger.)
Thou shalt not die! I swear I love thee still:
That secret sympathy which long has bound us
Pleads for thy life with sweet but strong entreaty.
Thou shalt repair the wrongs of that dear saint,
And be again my friend.

ORLANDO
Oh, hear me.

EMMELINA
No.
I cannot stoop to live on charity,
And what but charity is love compell'd?
I've been a weak, a fond, believing woman,
And credulous beyond my sex's softness:
But with the weakness, I've the pride of woman.
I lov'd with virtue, but I fondly lov'd;
That passion fix'd my fate, determin'd all,
And mark'd at once the colour of my life.
Hearts that love well, love long; they love but once.
My peace thou hast destroy'd, my honour's mine:
She who aspir'd to gain Orlando's heart
Shall never owe Orlando's hand to pity.

[Exit **EMMELINA**.

ORLANDO (after a pause.)
And I still live!

RIVERS

Farewell! should I stay longer
I might forget my vow.

ORLANDO
Yet hear me, Rivers.

[Exit **RIVERS, ORLANDO** following.

[Enter **BERTRAND** on the other side.

BERTRAND
How's this? my fortune fails me, both alive!
I thought by stirring Rivers to this quarrel,
There was at least an equal chance against him.
I work invisibly, and like the tempter
My agency is seen in its effects.
Well, honest Bertrand! now for Julia's letter.

[Takes out a letter.

This fond epistle of a love-sick maid,
I've sworn to give, but did not swear to whom.
"Give it my love," said she, "my dearest lord!"
Rivers she meant; there's no address—that's lucky.
Then where's the harm? Orlando is a lord,
As well as Rivers, loves her, too, as well.

[Breaks open the letter.

I must admire your style—your pardon, fair one.

[Runs over it.

I tread in air—methinks I brush the stars,
And spurn the subject world which rolls beneath me.—
There's not a word but fits Orlando's case
As well as Rivers';—tender to excess—
No name—'twill do; his faith in me is boundless;
Then, as the brave are still, he's unsuspecting,
And credulous beyond a woman's weakness.

[Going out, he spies the dagger.

Orlando's dagger!—ha! 'tis greatly thought.
This may do noble service; such a scheme!
My genius catches fire! the bright idea
Is form'd at once, and fit for instant action!

[Exit.

SCENE—The Garden

BERTRAND
'Twas here we were to meet; where does he stay?
This compound of strange contradicting parts,
Too flexible for virtue, yet too virtuous
To make a flourishing, successful villain.
Conscience! be still; preach not remorse to me;
Remorse is for the luckless, failing villain.
He who succeeds repents not; penitence
Is but another name for ill success.
Was Nero penitent when Rome was burnt?
No: but had Nero been a petty villain,
Subject to laws and liable to fear,
Nero perchance had been a penitent.
He comes:—this paper makes him all my own.

[Enter **ORLANDO**.

ORLANDO
At length this wretched, tempest-beaten bark
Seems to have found its haven: I'm resolv'd;
My wav'ring principles are fix'd to honour;
My virtue gathers force, my mind grows strong,
I feel an honest confidence within,
A precious earnest of returning peace.

BERTRAND
Who feels secure stands on the verge of ruin. [Aside.
Trust me, it joys my heart to see you thus:
What have I not attempted for your sake!
My love for you has warp'd my honest nature,
And friendship has infring'd on higher duties.

ORLANDO
It was a generous fault.

BERTRAND
Yet 'twas a fault.
Oh, for a flinty heart that knows no weakness,
But moves right onward, unseduc'd by friendship,
And all the weak affections!

ORLANDO
Hear me, Bertrand!
This is my last farewell; absence alone
Can prop my stagg'ring virtue.

BERTRAND
You're resolv'd:
Then Julia's favours come too late.

ORLANDO
What favours?

BERTRAND
Nay, nothing; I renounce these weak affections;
They have misled us both. I, too, repent,
And will return the letter back to Julia.

ORLANDO
Letter! what letter? Julia write to me?
I will not see it.—What would Rivers say?
Bertrand! he sav'd my life:—I will not see it.

BERTRAND
I do not mean you should; nay, I refus'd
To bring it you.

ORLANDO
Refus'd to bring the letter?

BERTRAND
Yes, I refus'd at first.

ORLANDO
Then thou hast brought it?
My faithful Bertrand!—come.

BERTRAND
'Twere best not see it.

ORLANDO
Not see it! how! not read my Julia's letter!
An empire should not bribe me to forbear.
Come, come.

BERTRAND
Alas, how frail is human virtue!
My resolution melts, and though I mean not

To trust you with the letter, I must tell you
With what a thousand, thousand charms she gave it.
"Take this," said she, "and as Orlando reads it,
Attend to every accent of his voice;
Watch every little motion of his eye;
Mark if it sparkles when he talks of Julia;
If when he speaks, poor Julia be the theme;
If when he sighs, his bosom heave for Julia:
Note every trifling act, each little look,
For, oh! of what importance is the least
To those who love like me!"

ORLANDO
Delicious poison!
O how it taints my soul! give me the letter.

[**BERTRAND** offers it, **ORLANDO** refuses.

Ha! where's the virtue which but now I boasted?
'Tis lost, 'tis gone—conflicting passions tear me.
I am again a villain.—Give it—no;
A spark of honour strikes upon my soul.
Take back the letter; take it back, good Bertrand!
Spite of myself compel me to be just:
I will not read it.

BERTRAND
How your friend will thank you!
Another day makes Julia his for ever.
Even now the great pavilion is prepar'd;
There will the nuptial rites be solemnis'd.
Julia already dress'd in bridal robes
Like some fair victim—

ORLANDO
O, no more, no more.
What can she write to me?

BERTRAND
Some prudent counsel.

ORLANDO
Then wherefore fear to read it? come, I'll venture:
What wondrous harm can one poor letter do?
The letter—quick the letter.

BERTRAND
Since you force me.

[Gives it.

ORLANDO
Be firm, ye shivering nerves! It is her hand.
(Reads.) "To spare my blushes Bertrand brings you this.
How have you wrong'd me! you believ'd me false;
'Twas my compassion for your friend deceiv'd you.
Meet me at midnight in the great pavilion;
But shun till then my presence; from that hour
My future life is yours; your once-lov'd friend
I pity and esteem; but you alone
Possess the heart of Julia."
This to me!
I dream, I rave, 'tis all Elysium round me,
And thou, my better angel! this to me!

BERTRAND
I'm dumb: oh, Julia! what a fall is thine!

ORLANDO
What! is it such a crime to love? away—
Thy moral comes too late; thou shouldst have urg'd
Thy scruple sooner, or not urg'd at all:
Thou shouldst—alas! I know not what I say—
But this I know, the charming Julia loves me,
Appoints a meeting at the dead of night!
She loves! The rest is all beneath my care.

BERTRAND
Be circumspect; the hour is just at hand;
Since all is ready for your purpos'd parting,
See your attendants be dispos'd aright,
Near the pavilion gate.

ORLANDO
Why so?

BERTRAND
'Tis plain
Julia must be the partner of your flight:
'Tis what she means, you must not mind her struggles;
A little gentle violence perhaps,
To make her yield to what she had resolv'd,
And save her pride; she'll thank you for it after.

ORLANDO
Take her by force? I like not that: O Bertrand,

There is a mutinous spirit in my blood,
That wars against my conscience.—Tell my Julia
I will not fail to meet her.

BERTRAND
I obey.
Be near the garden: I shall soon return.

[Exit **BERTRAND**.

ORLANDO
This giant sin, whose bulk so lately scar'd me,
Shrinks to a common size; I now embrace
What I but lately fear'd to look upon.
Why, what a progress have I made in guilt!
Where is the hideous form it lately wore?
It grows familiar to me; I can think,
Contrive, and calmly meditate on mischief;
Talk temp'rately of sin, and cherish crimes
I lately so abhorr'd, that had they once
But glanc'd upon the surface of my fancy,
I had been terrified. Oh, wayward conscience!
Too tender for repose, to sear'd for penitence!

[Exit **ORLANDO**.

SCENE—Another Part of the Garden

A grand pavilion—The moon shining.

[Enter **RIVERS** in a melancholy attitude.

RIVERS
Ye lovely scenes of long remember'd bliss!
Scenes which I hop'd were fated to bestow
Still dearer blessings in a beauteous bride!
Thou gay pavilion, which art dress'd so fair
To witness my espousals, why, ah! why
Art thou adorn'd in vain? Yet still I haunt thee,
For Julia lov'd thee once:—dear faithless Julia!
Yet is she false? Orlando swore she was not:
It may be so; yet she avoids my presence,
Keeps close from every eye, but most from mine.

[Enter **ORLANDO**.

ORLANDO
Ha! Rivers here! would I had shunn'd his walks!
How shall I meet the man I mean to wrong?

RIVERS
Why does Orlando thus expose his health
To this cold air?

ORLANDO
I ask the same of Rivers?

RIVERS
Because this solitude, this silent hour,
Feeds melancholy thoughts, and soothes my soul.
My Julia will not see me.

ORLANDO
How?

RIVERS
She denies me
Admittance to her presence.

ORLANDO (aside.)
Then I'm lost,
Confirm'd a villain; now 'tis plain she loves me.

RIVERS
She will not pardon me one single fault
Of jealous love, though thou hadst clear'd up all.

ORLANDO
Wait till to-morrow, all will then be known.

RIVERS
Wait till to-morrow? Look at that pavilion;
All was prepar'd: yes, I dare tell thee all,
For thou art honest now.

ORLANDO (aside.)
That wounds too deeply.

RIVERS
Soon as the midnight bell gave the glad summons,
This dear pavilion had beheld her mine.

ORLANDO
All will be well to-morrow.—(Aside.) If I stay

I shall betray the whole.—Good night, my Rivers.

RIVERS
Good night; go you to rest; I still shall walk.

[Exit **ORLANDO**.

RIVERS
Yes, I will trace her haunts; my too fond heart,
Like a poor bird that's hunted from its nest,
Dares not return, and knows not where to fix;
Still it delights to hover round the spot
Which lately held its treasure; eyes it still,
And with heart-breaking tenderness surveys
The scene of joys which never may return.

[Exit.

SCENE—Another Part of the Garden

[Re-enter **ORLANDO**.

ORLANDO
Did he say rest? talk'd he of rest to me?
Can rest and guilt associate? but no matter,
I cannot now go back; then such a prize,
Such voluntary love, so fair, so yielding,
Would make archangels forfeit their allegiance!
I dare not think: reflection leads to madness.

[Enter **BERTRAND**.

Bertrand! I was not made for this dark work;
My heart recoils—poor Rivers!

BERTRAND
What of Rivers?

ORLANDO
I've seen him.

BERTRAND
Where?

ORLANDO
Before the great pavilion.

BERTRAND

(aside.) That's lucky, saves me trouble: were he absent,
Half of my scheme had fail'd.

ORLANDO

He's most unhappy;
He wish'd me rest, spoke kindly to me, Bertrand;
How, how can I betray him?

BERTRAND

He deceives you;
He's on the watch, else wherefore now abroad
At this late hour? beware of treachery.

ORLANDO

I am myself the traitor.

BERTRAND

Come, no more!
The time draws near, you know the cypress walk,
'Tis dark.

ORLANDO

The fitter for dark deeds like mine.

BERTRAND

I have prepar'd your men; when the bell strikes,
Go into the pavilion; there you'll find
The blushing maid, who with faint screams, perhaps,
Will feign resentment. But you want a sword.

ORLANDO

A sword!—I'll murder no one—why a sword?

BERTRAND

'Tis prudent to be arm'd;—no words,—take mine;
There may be danger,—Julia may be lost,—
This night secures or loses her for ever.
The cypress walk—spare none who look like spies.

ORLANDO (looking at the sword.)
How deeply is that soul involv'd in guilt,
Who dares not hold communion with its thoughts,
Nor ask itself what it designs to do!
But dallies blindly with the gen'ral sin
Of unexamin'd, undefin'd perdition!

[Exit **ORLANDO**.

BERTRAND
Thus far propitious fortune fills my sails;
Yet still I doubt his milkiness of soul;
My next exploit must be to find out Rivers,
And, as from Julia, give him a feign'd message,
To join her here at the pavilion gate;
There shall Orlando's well-arm'd servants meet him,
And take his righteous soul from this bad world.
If they should fail, his honest cousin Bertrand
Will help him onward in his way to heav'n.
Then this good dagger, which I'll leave beside him,
Will, while it proves the deed, conceal the doer.
'Tis not an English instrument of mischief,
And who'll suspect good Bertrand wore a dagger?
To clear me further, I've no sword—unarm'd—
Poor helpless Bertrand! Then no longer poor,
But Guildford's heir, and lord of these fair lands.

[Exit **BERTRAND**.

[Enter **ORLANDO** on the other side.

ORLANDO
Draw thy dun curtain round, oh, night! black night!
Inspirer and concealer of foul crimes!
Thou wizard night! who conjur'st up dark thoughts,
And mak'st him bold who else would start at guilt!
Beneath thy veil the villain dares to act
What, in broad day, he would not dare to think.
Oh, night! thou hid'st the dagger's point from men,
But canst thou screen the assassin from himself?
Shut out the eye of heaven? extinguish conscience?
Or heal the wounds of honour? Oh, no, no, no!
Yonder she goes—the guilty, charming Julia!
My genius drives me on—Julia, I come.

[Runs off.

SCENE—The Pavilion

An arch'd door, through which **JULIA** and her **MAID** come forward on the Stage.

JULIA
Not here? not come? look out my faithful Anna.

There was a time—oh, time for ever dear!
When Rivers would not make his Julia wait.
Perhaps he blames me, thinks the appointment bold,
Too daring, too unlike his bashful Julia;
But 'twas the only means my faithful love
Devis'd to save him from Orlando's rashness.
I have kept close, refus'd to see my Rivers;
Now all is still, and I have ventur'd forth,
With this kind maid and virtue for my guard.
Come, we'll go in, he cannot sure be long.
[They go into the pavilion.

[Enter **ORLANDO**, his sword drawn and bloody, his hair dishevelled.

ORLANDO
What have I done? a deed that earns damnation!
Where shall I fly? ah! the pavilion door!
'Tis open—it invites me to fresh guilt;
I'll not go in—let that fall'n angel wait,
And curse her stars as I do.

[The midnight bell strikes.

Hark! the bell!
Demons of darkness, what a peal is that!
Again! 'twill wake the dead—I cannot bear it!
'Tis terrible as the last trumpet's sound!
That was the marriage signal! Powers of hell,
What blessings have I blasted! Rivers!—Julia!

[**JULIA** comes out.

JULIA
My Rivers calls; I come, I come.—Orlando!

ORLANDO
Yes,
Thou beautiful deceiver! 'tis that wretch.

JULIA
That perjur'd friend.

ORLANDO
That devil!

JULIA
I'm betray'd.
Why art thou here?

ORLANDO
Thou canst make ruin lovely,
Or I would ask, why dost thou bring me here?

JULIA
I bring thee here?

ORLANDO
Yes, thou, bright falsehood! thou.

JULIA
No, by my hopes of heaven! where is my Rivers?
Some crime is meant.

ORLANDO (catches her hand.)
Julia! the crime is done.
Dost thou not shudder? art thou not amaz'd?
Art thou not cold and blasted with my touch?
Is not thy blood congeal'd? does no black horror
Fill thy presaging soul? look at these hands;
Julia! they're stain'd with blood; blood, Julia, blood!
Nay, look upon them.

JULIA
Ah! I dare not.—Blood!

ORLANDO
Yes, thou dear false one, with the noblest blood
That ever stain'd a dark assassin's hand.
Had not thy letter, with the guilty message
To meet thee here this hour, blinded my honour,
And wrought my passion into burning frenzy,
Whole worlds should not have bribed me.

JULIA
Letter and message?
I sent thee none.

ORLANDO
Then Bertrand has betray'd me!
And I have done a deed beyond all reach,
All hope of mercy—I have murder'd Rivers.

JULIA
Oh! [She falls into her maid's arms.

ORLANDO

O rich reward which Love prepares for Murder!
Thus hell repays its instruments!

[Enter **GUILDFORD** with servants.

GUILFORD
Where is he?
Where is this midnight murderer? this assassin?
This is the place Orlando's servant nam'd.

ORLANDO
The storm comes on. 'Tis Guildford, good old man!
Behold the wretch accurst of heaven and thee.

GUILFORD
Accurst of both, indeed. How, Julia fainting!

ORLANDO
She's pure as holy truth; she was deceiv'd,
And so was I.

GUILFORD
Who tempted thee to this?

ORLANDO
Love, hell, and Bertrand.

JULIA (recovering.)
Give me back my Rivers;
I will not live without him.—Oh, my father!

GUILFORD
Father! I am none; I am no more a father;
I have no child; my son is basely murder'd,
And my sweet daughter, at the fatal news,
Is quite bereft of reason.

ORLANDO
Seize me, bind me:
If death's too great a mercy, let me live:
Drag me to some damp dungeon's horrid gloom,
Deep as the centre, dark as my offences;
Come, do your office, take my sword: oh, Bertrand,
Yet, ere I perish, could it reach thy heart!

[They seize **ORLANDO**.

JULIA

I will not long survive thee, oh, my Rivers!

[Enter **RIVERS** with the dagger.

RIVERS
Who calls on Rivers with a voice so sad,
So full of sweetness?

GUILFORD
Ah, my son!

JULIA
'Tis he, 'tis he!

[**JULIA** and **RIVERS** run into each other's arms.

[**ORLANDO** breaks from the guards and falls on his knees.

ORLANDO
He lives, he lives! the god-like Rivers lives!
Hear it, ye host of heaven! witness, ye saints!
Recording angels, tell it in your songs;
Breathe it, celestial spirits, to your lutes,
That Rivers lives!

JULIA
Explain this wond'rous happiness?

RIVERS
'Twas Bertrand whom Orlando killed; the traitor
Has with his dying breath confess'd the whole.

ORLANDO
Good sword, I thank thee!

RIVERS
In the tangled maze
Orlando miss'd the path he was to take,
And pass'd through that where Bertrand lay conceal'd
To watch th' event: Orlando thought 'twas me,
And that I play'd him false: the walk was dark.
In Bertrand's bloody hand I found this dagger,
With which he meant to take my life; but how
Were you alarm'd?

GUILFORD
One of Orlando's men,
Whom wealth could never bribe to join in murder—

ORLANDO
Murder! I bribe to murder?

RIVERS
No; 'twas Bertrand
Brib'd them to that curs'd deed: he lov'd my sister.

ORLANDO
Exquisite villain!

GUILFORD
Fly to Emmelina,
If any spark of reason yet remain,
Tell her the joyful news.—Alas, she's here!
Wildly she flies!—Ah, my distracted child!

[Enter **EMMELINA** distracted.

EMMELINA
Off, off! I will have way! ye shall not hold me:
I come to seek my Lord: is he not here?
Tell me, ye virgins, have ye seen my love,
Or know you where his flocks repose at noon?
My love is comely—sure you must have seen him;
'Tis the great promiser! who vows and swears;
The perjur'd youth! who deals in oaths and breaks them.
In truth he might deceive a wiser maid.
I lov'd him once; he then was innocent:
He was no murderer then, indeed he was not;
He had not kill'd my brother.

RIVERS
Nor has now;
Thy brother lives.

EMMELINA
I know it—yes, he lives
Among the cherubim. Murd'rers too will live:
But where? I'll tell you where—down, down, down, down.
How deep it is! 'tis fathomless—'tis dark!
No—there's a pale blue flame—ah, poor Orlando!

GUILFORD
My heart will burst.

ORLANDO
Pierce mine, and that will ease it.

EMMELINA (comes up to her father.)
I knew a maid who lov'd—but she was mad—
Fond, foolish girl! Thank heav'n, I am not mad;
Yet the afflicting angel has been with me;
But do not tell my father, he would grieve;
Sweet, good old man—perhaps he'd weep to hear it:
I never saw my father weep but once;
I'll tell you when it was—I did not weep;
'Twas when—but soft, my brother must not know it,
'Twas when his poor fond daughter was refus'd.

GUILFORD
Who can bear this?

ORLANDO
I will not live to bear it.

EMMELINA (comes up to **ORLANDO**)
Take comfort, thou poor wretch! I'll not appear
Against thee, nor shall Rivers; but blood must,
Blood will appear; there's no concealing blood.
What's that? my brother's ghost—it vanishes:

[Catches hold of **RIVERS**.

Stay, take me with thee, take me to the skies;
I have thee fast: thou shalt not go without me.
But hold—may we not take the murd'rer with us?
That look says—No. Why then I'll not go with thee.
Yet hold me fast—'tis dark—I'm lost—I'm gone.

[Dies.

ORLANDO
One crime makes many needful: this day's sin
Blots out a life of virtue. Good old man!
My bosom bleeds for thee; thy child is dead,
And I the cause. 'Tis but a poor atonement;
But I can make no other.

[Stabs himself.

RIVERS
What hast thou done?

ORLANDO
Fill'd up the measure of my sins. Oh, mercy!

Eternal goodness, pardon this last guilt!
Rivers, thy hand!—farewell! forgive me, Heaven!
Yet is it not an act which bars forgiveness,
And shuts the door of grace for ever!—Oh!

[Dies.

[The curtain fails to soft music.

EPILOGUE

Unhand me, gentlemen; by Heaven, I say,
I'll make a ghost of him who bars my way.

[Behind the scenes.

Forth let me come—A Poetaster true,
As lean as Envy, and as baneful too;
On the dull audience let me vent my rage,
Or drive these female scribblers from the stage.
For scene or History, we've none but these,
The law of Liberty and Wit they seize;
In Tragic—Comic—Pastoral—they dare to please.
Each puny Bard must surely burst with spite,
To find that women with such fame can write:
But, oh, your partial favour is the cause,
Which feeds their follies with such full applause.
Yet still our tribe shall seek to blast their fame,
And ridicule each fair pretender's aim;
Where the dull duties of domestic life,
Wage with the Muse's toils eternal strife.
What motley cares Corilla's mind perplex,
While maids and metaphors conspire to vex!
In studious dishabille behold her sit,
A letter'd gossip, and a housewife wit;
At once invoking, though for different views,
Her gods, her cook, her milliner and muse,
Round her strew'd room a frippery chaos lies,
A chequer'd wreck of notable and wise;
Bills, books, caps, couplets, combs, a vary'd mass,
Oppress the toilet, and obscure the glass;
Unfinish'd here an epigram is laid,
And there, a mantua-maker's bill unpaid;
Here, new-born plays foretaste the town's applause,
There, dormant patterns pine for future gauze;
A moral essay now is all her care,

A satire next, and then a bill of fare:
A scene she now projects, and now a dish,
Here's act the first—and here—remove with fish.
Now while this eye in a fine frenzy rolls,
That, soberly casts up a bill for coals;
Black pins and daggers in one leaf she sticks,
And tears, and thread, and balls, and thimbles mix.
Sappho, 'tis true, long vers'd in epic song,
For years esteem'd all household studies wrong;
When, dire mishap, though neither shame nor sin,
Sappho herself, and not her muse, lies in.
The virgin Nine in terror fly the bower,
And matron Juno claims despotic power;
Soon Gothic hags the classic pile o'erturn,
A caudle-cup supplants the sacred urn;
Nor books, nor implements escape their rage,
They spike the ink-stand, and they rend the page;
Poems and plays one barbarous fate partake,
Ovid and Plautus suffer at the stake,
And Aristotle's only sav'd—to wrap plum-cake.
Yet, shall a woman tempt the tragic scene?
And dare—but hold—I must repress my spleen;
I see your hearts are pledg'd to her applause,
While Shakspeare's spirit seems to aid her cause;
Well pleas'd to aid—since o'er his sacred bier
A female hand did ample trophies rear,
And gave the greenest laurel that is worshipp'd there.

Hannah More - A Short Biography

Hannah More was born on February 2nd, 1745 at Fishponds in the parish of Stapleton, near Bristol. She was the fourth of five daughters of Jacob More, a schoolmaster. He was originally from a family of Presbyterians in Norfolk, but had become a member of the Church of England to pursue a career in the Church. After losing a lawsuit over an estate he had hoped to inherit, he moved to Bristol, becoming an excise officer and later a teacher at the Fishponds free school.

The City of Bristol, at that time, was a centre for slave-trading and Hannah would, over time, become one of its staunchest critics.

The More's were a close family and all the sisters were educated at first by their father who taught them Latin and mathematics. Hannah was also taught French by her elder sisters. Her conversational French was improved by time spent with French prisoners of war from the Seven-Year's-War in Frenchay, then a small village near Bristol.

She was keen to learn, possessed a sharp intellect and was assiduous in studying and, according to family tradition, began writing at an early age.

In 1758 Jacob established his own girls' boarding school at Trinity Street in Bristol for the elder sisters, Mary and Elizabeth, to run. Hannah became a pupil there when she was 12. Jacob and his wife moved to Stony Hill in the city to open a school for boys.

Hannah became a teacher at her sister's school and it was here that she produced her first literary efforts. These were prompted by trying to find material suitable for her young charges to act in. Her first, written in 1762, was The Search after Happiness (by the mid-1780s some 10,000 copies had been sold).

In 1767 Hannah gave up her share in the school to become engaged to William Turner. After six years, with no wedding in sight, and Turner reluctant to move forward, the engagement was broken off. It was now 1773 and by all accounts Hannah suffered a nervous breakdown and spent some time recuperating in nearby Uphill. Turner then bestowed upon her an annual annuity of £200. This was enough to meet her needs and set her free to pursue a literary career. With that ambition London was her next stop. She travelled there in the winter of 1773/74 together with her sisters, Sarah and Martha.

She had previously written some verses on a production of King Lear staged by the famous actor David Garrick and this led to a lasting friendship with him and a pivotal introduction to the London Literary society. Now she met and charmed Samuel Johnson, Joshua Reynolds and Edmund Burke. Johnson is quoted as saying to her "Madam, before you flatter a man so grossly to his face, you should consider whether or not your flattery is worth having." He would later be quoted as calling her "the finest versifatrix in the English language".

Hannah also became a leading member of the Bluestocking group of women who met to further literary and intellectual pursuits. Here she met women who were to become life-long friends; Elizabeth Montagu, Frances Boscawen, Elizabeth Carter, Elizabeth Vesey and Hester Chapone (Hannah later wrote a celebration of this circle in her 1782 poem The Bas Bleu, or, Conversation, published in 1784).

Her first play, The Inflexible Captive, was staged at Bath in 1775. It was based on the opera, Attilio Regulo, by the Italian Pietro Metastasio (1698-1782) whose works she admired.

Her theatrical career was now in full swing. David Garrick himself produced her next play, Percy, in 1777 as well as writing both the Prologue and Epilogue for it. It was a great success when performed at Covent Garden in December of that year. Her next play, Fatal Falsehood, was staged in 1779, shortly after the death of Garrick. It was less successful but still admired.

With David Garrick now passed (January 20th, 1779) Hannah came to view the theatre as both morally wrong and not where her ambitions now lay. She now began to spend her time advancing her interests in other areas.

In 1781 she first met Horace Walpole, man of letters art historian and Whig politician and now corresponded regularly with him.

A friendship with James Oglethorpe, who had long been concerned with slavery as a moral issue and who was working with Granville Sharp in an early abolitionist capacity, started to awaken Hannah's social conscious.

Hannah turned to religious writing, beginning with her Sacred Dramas in 1782; it rapidly ran through nineteen editions. These and the poems Bas-Bleu and Florio (1786) mark her gradual transition to a more serious and considered view of life and are fully expressed in her Thoughts on the Importance of the Manners of the Great to General Society (1788), and An Estimate of the Religion of the Fashionable World (1790).

In Bristol, in 1784, she discovered the poet Ann Yearsley, the so-called 'poetical milkmaid of Bristol'. With Yearsley destitute, Hannah raised a considerable sum of money for her. Lactilia, as Yearsley was known, published Poems, on Several Occasions in 1785, earning about £600. Hannah and Elizabeth Montagu held the profits in trust to protect them from Yearsley's husband. However Ann wished for the capital to be made over, and made insinuations of stealing against Hannah. The money was released and Hannah felt her reputation had been tarnished.

With the death of Samuel Johnson in December 1784, Hannah moved, with her sister Martha, in 1795, to a cottage at Cowslip Green, near Wrington in rural Somerset, "to escape from the world gradually".

In the summer of 1786, she spent time with Sir Charles and Lady Margaret Middleton at their home in Teston in Kent. Among their guests was the local vicar James Ramsay and a young Thomas Clarkson, both of whom were central to the early abolition campaign against slavery.

In 1787, she met John Newton and the 'Clapham Sect' (a group of wealthy evangelical Christians who lived near Clapham and met at Henry Thornton's house). The group was strongly opposed to the Slave Trade. William Wilberforce was a member of the group and he and Hannah became firm friends.

Hannah contributed much to the running of the newly-founded Abolition Society including, in February 1788, her publication of Slavery, a Poem which has long been recognised as one of the most important poems of the abolition period. The poem dramatically described a mistreated, enslaved female separated from her children and severely questioned Britain's role in the Slave Trade.

Her relationship with members of the society, especially Wilberforce, was close. She spent the summer of 1789 holidaying with Wilberforce in the Peak District, planning for the abolition campaign, which, at the time, was at its height.

Her work now became more evangelical. In the 1790s she wrote several Cheap Repository Tracts which covered moral, religious and political topics and were both for sale or distributed to literate poor people. This coincided with her increasing philanthropic work in the Mendip area.

Beyond any doubt, Hannah was the most influential female member of the Society for Effecting the Abolition of the African Slave Trade.

Hannah wrote many ethical books and tracts: Strictures on the Modern System of Female Education (1799), Hints towards Forming the Character of a Young Princess (1805), Cœlebs in Search of a Wife (only nominally a story, 1809), Practical Piety (1811), Christian Morals (1813), Character of St Paul (1815), Moral Sketches (1819). She was a rapid writer, and her work is consequently discursive, animated and without a rigorous structure.

However the originality and force of Hannah's writings perhaps explains her extraordinary popularity. At the behest of Beilby Porteus, Bishop of London and a leading abolitionist, Hannah wrote many spirited rhymes and prose tales, the earliest of which was Village Politics, by Will Chip (1792), intended to counteract the doctrines of Thomas Paine and the influence of the French Revolution.

The series of Cheap Repository Tracts, eventually led to the formation of the Religious Tracts Society. The Tracts were produced at the rate of three a month between 1795 and 1797.

The most famous is perhaps The Shepherd of Salisbury Plain, describing a family of incredible frugality and contentment. Two million copies of these rapid and telling sketches were circulated, in one year, teaching the poor in rhetoric of the most ingenious homeliness to rely upon the virtues of content, sobriety, humility, industry and reverence for the British Constitution, hatred of the French, trust in God and in the kindness of the gentry.

Several of the Tracts oppose slavery and the slave trade, in particular, the poem The Sorrows of Yamba; or, The Negro Woman's Lamentation, which appeared in November 1795 and which was co-authored with Eaglesfield Smith. However, the tracts have also been noted for their encouragement of social quietism in an age of revolution.

In 1789, she purchased a small house at Cowslip Green in Somerset. Wilberforce encouraged Hannah to set up a Sunday school in Cheddar, where poor children could be taught to read. Soon she and her sisters had set up similar schools throughout the Mendip villages, despite fierce opposition.

She was instrumental in setting up twelve schools by 1800 where reading, the Bible and the catechism were taught to local children. Hannah also donated money to Bishop Philander Chase for the founding of Kenyon College, and a portrait of her hangs there in Peirce Hall.

John Scandrett Harford of Blaise Castle was a prodigious benefactor to More's schools in the 1790s, and Hannah modeled the idealised hero and heroine in Cœlebs in Search of Wife (1809) on Mr and Mrs Harford.

However it cannot be said that Hannah was a staunch supporter of Women's rights. She refused to read Mary Wollstonecraft's Rights of Women, saying "so many women are fond of government... because they are not fit for it. To be unstable and capricious is but too characteristic of our sex". She was also shocked by the movement for female education in France, saying "they run to study philosophy, and neglect their families to be present at lectures in anatomy". She is also said to have turned down an honorary membership of the Royal Society of Literature because she considered her "sex alone a disqualification".

The More sisters also met with a good deal of opposition in their philanthropic works: the farmers thought that education, even to the limited extent of learning to read, would be fatal to agriculture, and the clergy, whose neglect she was making good, accused her of Methodist tendencies.

She continued to oppose slavery throughout her life, but at the time of the Abolition Bill of 1807 (which outlawed the slave trade, but not slavery itself), her health did not permit her to take as active a role in the movement as she had done in the late 1780s, although she maintained a correspondence with Wilberforce and others Abolitionists.

In her later life, she continued to dedicate much of her time to religious writing. Nevertheless, her most popular work was a novel, Cœlebs in Search of a Wife, which appeared in two volumes in 1809 (and which ran to nine editions in 1809 alone).

In 1816, Hannah was still at odds with the French. Following Waterloo she is quoted as saying that 'peace with France is a worse evil than war', and refused to allow a French translation of Cœlebs.

Her last few years were spent at Clifton, people from all parts came to visit her even though her health was fading and she was writing less often.

She lived just long enough to see the act finally abolishing slavery. In July 1833, the Bill to abolish slavery throughout the British Empire passed in the House of Commons, followed by the House of Lords on August 1st.

Hannah More died on September 7th, 1833. She is buried at Church of All Saints, Wrington. In her will she left more than £30,000 to charities and religious societies, the equivalent today of many millions.

www.ingramcontent.com/pod-product-compliance
Lightning Source LLC
Chambersburg PA
CBHW060146050426
42448CB00010B/2322